Sorting with Snakes

By Mary Rose McDonnell

GS MATH

Please visit our website, www.garethstevens.com. For a free color catalog of all our high-quality books, call toll free 1-800-542-2595 or fax 1-877-542-2596.

Library of Congress Cataloging-in-Publication Data

McDonnell, Mary Rose.
Sorting with snakes / by Mary Rose McDonnell.
   p. cm. — (Animal math)
Includes index.
ISBN 978-1-4339-9329-9 (pbk.)
ISBN 978-1-4339-9330-5 (6-pack)
ISBN 978-1-4339-9328-2 (library binding)
1. Set theory—Juvenile literature. 2. Snakes—Juvenile literature. I. Title.
QA248.M33 2014
511.322—dc23

First Edition

Published in 2014 by
Gareth Stevens Publishing
111 East 14th Street, Suite 349
New York, NY 10003

Copyright © 2014 Gareth Stevens Publishing

Designer: Nicholas Domiano
Editor: Therese Shea

Photo credits: Cover, p. 1 Anthony Mercieca/Photo Researchers/Getty Images; pp. 4, 14 (moccasin snake) iStockphoto/Thinkstock.com; pp. 4, 12, 14, 20 (indigo snake) iStockphoto/Thinkstock.com; pp. 5, 6, 8, 11, 12, 18 iStockphoto/Thinkstock.com; p. 7 Patrick K. Campbell/Shutterstock.com; p. 9 Dennis Donohue/Shutterstock.com; p. 13 Heiko Kiera/Shutterstock.com; p. 14 (red-bellied snake) Gerald A DeBoer/Shutterstock.com, (garter snake, brown snake) Melinda Fawver/Shutterstock.com; p. 15 Matt Jeppson/Shutterstock.com; p. 16 (egyptian cobra) Eric Isselee/Shutterstock.com, (side view cobra) Hemera/Thinkstock.com; p. 17 Skynavin/Shutterstock.com; p. 18 (red tailed boa) Robert Eastman/Shutterstock.com; pp. 18 (tree boa up), 20 (South American rattlesnake) Eric Isselee/Shutterstock.com; p. 19 Design Pics/Thinkstock.com; p. 21 Photos.com/Thinkstock.com.

Printed in the United States of America

CPSIA compliance information: Batch #CS13GS: For further information contact Gareth Stevens, New York, New York at 1-800-542-2595.

Contents

Boldface words appear in the glossary.

So Many Snakes

Snakes are all kinds of colors. Some have spots. Some have stripes. Let's sort some snakes. Check your answers on page 22.

Which snake below doesn't belong?

5

Snake Bodies

A snake is covered with pieces of hard skin called scales. Snakes **shed** their skin as they grow.

Which snakes below belong in a group of striped snakes?

7

Snakes smell by opening their mouth! A snake's tongue helps it smell, too.

Which snake below is smelling?

All snakes have teeth. Some have long teeth called fangs. Snakes with fangs are **poisonous**!

Which words below tell about the snake on the next page?

snake with fangs   snake without fangs

11

On the Move

Snakes slither. They push, pull, and slide. Some snakes jump out of trees!

Which snake below is the same as the snake on the next page?

13

Snakes have bones. They can bend in many ways. They can **coil**. This is one way they keep warm!

How many snakes below are coiled?

15

Cobras

Cobras can make their neck flat.
They do this when they're scared.
It makes them taller, too. Cobras
have poisonous fangs.

Which cobra below is different from
the others?

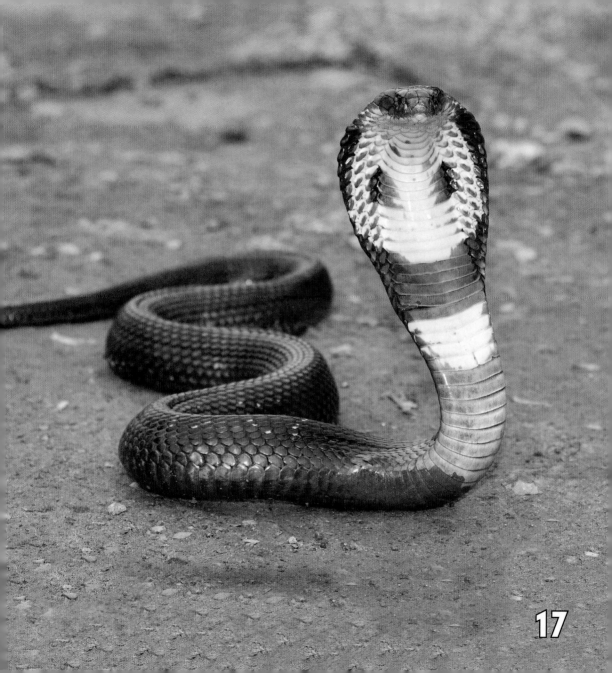

17

Boas

Boas are a group of snakes. Some are very thick. The green boa is very, very long!

Find the two green boas below.

Rattlesnakes

A rattlesnake's tail makes a noise. It tells us to stay away! Rattlesnakes have a poisonous bite.

Which snake below has a tail like the snake on the next page?

Glossary

coil: to curl around and around

poisonous: having poison, which causes illness or death

shed: to lose skin

Answer Key

page 4: black snake

page 6: snake at left, snake at right

page 8: snake at left

page 10: snake with fangs

page 12: snake at right

page 14: 3 coiled snakes

page 16: cobra at left

page 18: 2 green boas at left and right

page 20: snake at right

For More Information

Books

Bodden, Valerie. *Snakes.* Mankato, MN: Creative Education, 2010.

Rudy, Lisa Jo. *Snakes!* New York, NY: HarperCollins, 2005.

Stewart, Melissa. *Snakes!* Washington, DC: National Geographic, 2009.

Websites

Photo Gallery: Snakes

animals.nationalgeographic.com/animals/photos/snakes/
Check out amazing photos of snakes.

Snakes

www.kidzone.ws/lw/snakes/index.htm
Read fun facts about snakes.

Index